Easy wine guide
Portugal

Miguel Dias

Table of Contents

Welcome to the sunny side of wine _____ *1*

*Grape varieties*_____ *3*
   White grapes...7
   Red grapes 9

*The DOC System*_____ *11*

Top 7 wine regions _____ *13*
*1. Vinho Verde*_____ · _____ *14*
   Wine trails...16
   Beyond wine...24
*2. Douro*_____ *26*
   Port Wine...28
   Wine trails...35
   Port wine cellars 42
   Beyond wine...47
*3. Dão & Bairrada*_____ *49*
   Wine trails...52
   Beyond Wine...59

4. Lisboa & Tejo _____ *61*
    Wine Trails.. 65
    Beyond wine 72
5. Setúbal _____ *74*
    Wine trails 76
    Beyond wine 82
6. Alentejo _____ *85*
    Wine trails 87
    Beyond wine 95
7. Madeira _____ *97*
    Wine trails 100
    Beyond wine 108

Getting the most out of Portuguese Wine _____ *113*
Storing _____ *114*
Opening the Bottle _____ *116*
Serving _____ *119*
Tasting _____ *122*

Host a Wine Tasting Event _____ *125*

Final words _____ *129*
Bibliography _____ *133*
Notes to the reader _____ *136*
About the author _____ *133*

Welcome to the sunny side of wine

The Iberian Peninsula enjoys a long and diverse history as the crossroads between Europe and Africa. Many empires have dominated the region, from the Phoenicians to the Greeks, Romans, and Visigoths, leading to the Moorish conquest. Catholic monarchs ruled here, followed by a fascist regime in the twentieth century, and finally evolved into a republican democracy.

The wine legacy of Portugal reflects the region's deep and diverse cultural and geographical history. Ancient and modern sensibilities exist alongside in this magnificent part of the world, offering the opportunity to taste small production wines in regions that are, surprisingly, rarely visited. Combined with this traditional atmosphere, the region additionally provides sophisticated experiences with tasting rooms at spectacular wineries, exquisite restaurants, and even wine spas offering grape-based beauty treatments.

Portugal is the 11th largest wine producer in the world. Considering that the Portuguese territory is reasonably small, this is quite an accomplishment. There's no doubt that wine is an integral part of people's diet and socializing habits, explained by the average consumption of 72 bottles of wine per person per year!

Whether you are a wine connoisseur or merely beginning your wine adventures, this guide will assist you in diving into the exciting world of Portuguese wine culture.

Getting to know Portugal through its wines is the perfect way to connect with the rich culture of the region.

Grape varieties

The native grape varieties of Portugal are a national treasure! Exciting, distinct, prized, and savored by generations of Portuguese wine lovers, these wines are now ready to be discovered by international drinkers.

Portugal enjoys an impressive number of grape varieties, which provide character and uniqueness to the wines, distinguishing and highlighting them from a plethora of indistinct wines produced by dozens of countries around the world.

While French varieties and, to a lesser extent, Italian, German, and Spanish varieties have spread throughout the world, Portuguese varieties have remained isolated and limited to the national territory, in contrast to celebrity grapes like *Cabernet Sauvignon, Merlot, Syrah, Pinot Noir, Chardonnay, Sauvignon Blanc, Nebbiolo, Riesling*, or *Tempranillo*, which are widely grown across many wine-producing countries.

Even in Portugal, few varieties are identified by their names, aside from the *Alvarinho, Baga*, and *Touriga Nacional* trio, as there is little recognition among the more than 250 indigenous varieties officially registered, with names as exotic as *Esgana Cão* (Dog Strangler), *Amor-Não -Me-Deixes* (love-don't-leave-me), *Carrega Burros* (Donkey Loader), *Dedo de Dama* (Lady's Finger), or *Zé do Telheiro*.

In the vineyard, as in life, not all grape varieties are created equal, and not all regions are equally blessed. Among the homeland's DOs, two can be proud of receiving unrivaled recognition: the Douro and Vinho Verde. Douro grape varieties are presently widely known and valued by a legion of dedicated oenophiles, with references such as *Touriga Nacional, Touriga Franca, Tinta Roriz, Tinto Cão, Tinta Barroca, Sousão, Tinta Francisca, Gouveio, Rabigato, Viosinho,* and *Códega do Larinho*. In the Vinho Verde region, names remain with little awareness beyond *Alvarinho, Loureiro* and *Trajadura*.

Among the multiple top-quality grapes grown in Portugal, ten stand out, either alone or as part of a blend, to enhance Portugal's reputation for quality consistency and self-expression: *Alvarinho, Arinto (Pedernã), Encruzado,* and *Fernão Pires* are white varieties; *Baga, Castelo, Touriga Franca, Touriga Nacional, Trincadeira*, and *Tinta Roriz* are red varieties.

While I mention these single Portuguese varieties generically, the truth is the Portuguese wine tradition is based on a combination of grape varieties rather than the production of single-variety wines. There will invariably be exceptions to the rule, and one of the most notable is found in Bairrada, with its single-variety wines made from the *Baga* grape, which once held a near-monopoly in the region's red vine varieties. Another significant example comes from the region of Monção/Melgaço in Vinho Verde region, with its single-variety wines made from the *Alvarinho* grape that is rarely combined with any other type of grapes from the region. An exception is considered when the winemaker wants to create a wine with a light and fresh flavor, as in this instance the *Alvarinho* is blended with the *Trajadura* variety.

Portuguese winemakers employ the art of blending to balance the most favorable features that each variety can provide in a single wine. While some varieties add delicate fruit flavors, others add more body and roundness to the finish, resulting in a wine where the whole is better than the sum of its parts. This blending process is merely possible because of the abundance and diversity of Portuguese grape varieties, well adapted to the region's soils and climate. For example, in the Minho region, it can rain almost every day, which contrasts with parts of Alentejo and Douro Superior, where a drop of rain is a rarity during most part of the year. Bairrada and Colares suffer from an extreme Atlantic Ocean influence with rainy and cool seasons, while Alentejo and Dão's climate can vary between Mediterranean and Continental with significant temperature variations between summer and winter, and between day and night.

And that is the reason why Portuguese grape varieties vary so much across the country. They must adapt to the geography and climate conditions of each region, a lengthy process that has taken centuries to complete.

White grapes

Alvarinho produces distinctive, rich, mineral white wines with predominant notes of peaches and citrus fruits. Occasionally you can also find aromas and flowers related to tropical fruits and flowers.

This high-quality white grape has long been prized in Portugal's northwestern region, and it is commonly planted in the northern part of the Vinho Verde region, between the rivers Lima and Minho, which form the border with Spain. Alvarinho wines are full-bodied and higher in alcohol than most Vinho Verde and are frequently bottled as a single variety and labeled as such. When first bottled, these wines are delicious, but they even can get better with age. Growers in other parts of Portugal have recognized Alvarinho's superiority, and the variety is gradually spreading south.

Arinto/Pedernã produces elegant, mineral white wines with apple and lemon flavors that are delicious when young and fresh but can gain complexity with age. It's a late-ripening grape with the added benefit of retaining its distinct freshness even in hot weather. It's no surprise that it's grown throughout the country, to add a crisp elegance to blends of other white varieties. This also works in the cool Vinho Verde region (known as *Pedernã*), where the high acidity is advantageous to produce sparkling wine.

Encruzado produces elegant, well-balanced, full-bodied whites with delicate floral and citric aromas, as well as an appealing mineral character. Encruzado is delicious in its pure, un-oaked form, but it equally responds favorably to oak fermentation or oak aging, resulting in well-structured wines that can mature and gain complexity over time.

It is most found in the Dão region in the country's center-north, either as a single variety or in blends - these are some of Portugal's most exciting white wines. Encruzado grapes retain their fresh acidity in the vineyard, even in hot conditions, and ripen to perfection without becoming overly sweet.

Fernão Pires is a grape variety that yield fruity, fragrant whites with a *Muscat* flavor. The taste of citric fruits and floral aromas are fresher when picked early for drinking the wine at a young age. It is equally employed to produce sparkling wines and can be harvested later to make sweet wines.

It is Portugal's most cultivated white grape and is widely grown throughout the country, particularly along the western coast in the regions of Setubal Peninsula, Tejo, Lisboa, and Bairrada.

Red grapes

Baga is a late-ripening grape producer of lean, tannic reds that are astringent while young, but nuanced as they age. Baga may produce generous, deep, red wines with cherry flavors when bottled in hotter years, or through expert ripening and winemaking. The wine can develop complex flavors of herbs, malt, cedar, and tobacco leaf as it ages. Its heartland is Bairrada, but it also grows elsewhere in the Beiras, including Dão. It's also used as a sparkling wine base.

Castelão is the most widely planted black grape in southern Portugal, it produces hard, elegant, raspberry-fruit wines with a cedar, cigar-box flavor. It's at its best in the Palmela region, south of Lisbon, on the Setubal peninsula.

Tinta Roriz and Aragonez are grapes that produce superb, delicate red wines with aromas of cherry fruits, plums, and blackberries, as well as firm tannins that age well. Tinta Roriz, as it is known in the north of Portugal, is one of the most significant grapes for Port and Douro wines, as well as the Dão area. It is called Aragonez in the Alentejo region and is commonly blended with other varieties like *Trincadeira*.

Touriga Franca is a variety that offer flowery tones and blackberry fruit, and that produces darkly colored, firm but rich aromatic wines. It is the most widely planted grape in the Douro Valley and one of the five official grapes for Port.

Touriga Nacional are grapes used to produce firm, richly colored wines with complex aromas and flavors reminiscent of violets, licorice, ripe blackcurrants, and raspberries, along with a subtle, herby hint of bergamot. It's a northern grape, by origin, but now it is used all over Portugal with the potential to produce wines that age well.

Tinta Amarela and *Trincadeira* varieties are employed to produce reds with wonderfully bright raspberry fruit, spicy, peppery, herbal flavors, and fresh acidity. This red grape can be found all over Portugal, particularly in arid and warm climates, although it thrives in the Alentejo. *Tinta Amarela* is the name given to this grape in the Douro region.

The DOC System

Portuguese wine regions established the DOC system when the country joined the European Union in 1986. The DOC replaced the *Região Demarcada* system, created in the early twentieth century and similar to the *Spanish Denominación de Origen (DO)*.

The DOC not only protects the designation of origin but also develops restrictions to ensure wines from a certain wine region meet high-quality requirements. Establishing an alcohol level range, specifying authorized grape types, and time for bottle or oak age are only a few of the requirements. To ensure conformity with DOC criteria, all producers are required to submit wine samples to a governing authority.

We can find two tiers in addition to the DOC designation: *Indicação de Provença Regulada (IPR)* and *Vinho Regional*. IPR stands for "in training" and identifies regions that have established their regulating bodies but have yet to build a globally identifiable brand for their wines. *Vinho Regional* belongs to the lower tier, which includes all wines that do not fall into one of the higher-grade categories.

Top 7 wine regions

1. **Vinho Verde**
2. **Douro**
3. **Dão & Bairrada**
4. **Lisboa**
5. **Setúbal**
6. **Alentejo**
7. **Madeira**

1. Vinho Verde

Vinho Verde comes from Portugal's largest wine area, situated in the northwest of the country, and bordered on the north by the Minho River and on the west by the Atlantic Ocean. Intense precipitation and mild temperatures throughout the year contribute to the region's "green atmosphere," which inspired the wine's name: Vinho Verde means "Green Wine" in English. This distinctive location produces a fresh, young, light, and aromatic white wine ideal for any occasion, as it pairs well with seafood, fish, salads, and even sushi. Due to ongoing training and increased excitement among growers, the quality of Vinho Verde has improved considerably in recent years.

The traditional method of growing vineyards on top of trees and pergolas is being gradually replaced by wired rows that allow grapes to become healthier due to better sun lighting and breeze exposure.

This DOC is divided into nine sub-regions, each named after a town or river: Monção and Melgaco, Cávado, Lima, Ave, Basto, Sousa, Baio, Amarante, and Paiva. Monção and Melgaço are in the northern part of the Vinho Verde region, which has lower rainfall and higher temperatures than the rest of the territory. Alvarinho is the most popular grape variety in this microclimate, producing a full-bodied dry wine with a complex and fresh aroma reminiscent of citrus fruits and peaches. Traveling south, you'll come across the sub-regions of Cávado, Lima, and Ave, which produce a fresh and aromatic wine, often with a citrus scent. *Loureiro, Arinto*, and *Trajadura* are the main grape varieties used here. The sub-regions of Basto, Sousa, and Baião also produce dry light wines with rich flavors and a "mineral presence" in the mouth. Finally, the sub-regions of Amarante and Paiva are known for their fresh, young, and highly aromatic red wines.

Wine trails

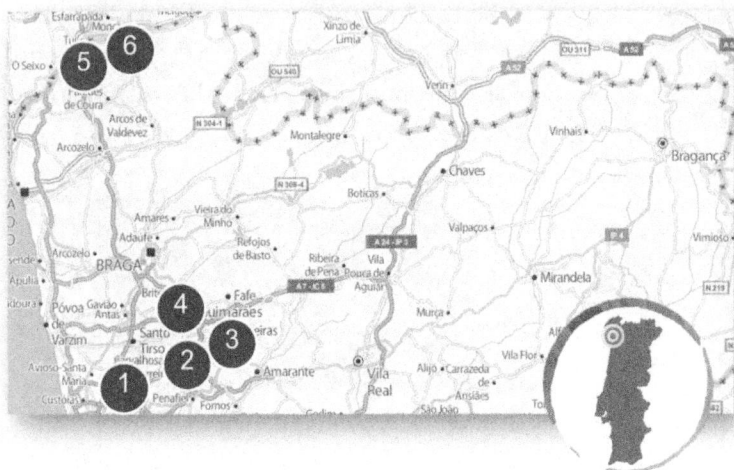

1. QUINTA DAS ARCAS
Tours | Trails | Shop
4440-392 Sobrado, Valongo
quintadasarcas.com

Quinta das Arcas is a company with approximately 140 hectares of vineyards spread across four properties, all planted with the best and most well-known varieties of the region: *Loureiro, Arinto, Trajadura, Alvarinho, Espadeiro,* and *Vinhão.*
Good agricultural practices combined with cutting-edge winemaking technology allow a distinct strategic positioning for

wine production in the region. All vineyards are grown using techniques that enable the protection of species and their habitats.

In addition, the company has a cheese production unit that makes artisanal cheese from the farm's milk.

2. QUINTA DA AVELEDA
Tours | Shop | Meals
Rua da Aveleda, 2, 4560-570 Penafiel
aveledaportugal.pt

The 205 hectares of vines at Aveleda stand at the heart of the Vinho Verde Demarcated Region. A visit to the cellar allows you to see the bottling process first-hand, followed by a wine and cheese tasting from their farm.

Aside from winemaking, the Quinta da Aveleda estate is well-known for its parks and gardens, where rare species of trees flourish, some of which have been around for over a hundred years. There was no surprise when the property received the "Architecture, Parks and Gardens Award" given by the International Best of Wine Tourism.

3. QUINTA DA LIXA
Hotel | Restaurant | SPA | Tours | Shop
Monte Vila Cova da Lixa, 4615-658 Lixa
quintadalixa.pt

Quinta da Lixa is one of the founders of the celebrated *Vinho Verde Route*. You can learn all about the winemaking and bottling processes with a visit to the winery or discover the grape varieties with the vineyard trail. Finally, you will have the opportunity to learn more about the various types of Quinta da Lixa wines during a wine tasting session led by the resident winemaker.

Quinta da Lixa also holds the hotel Monverde, an added value in the experience of enjoying the wine, culture, and surroundings of the region.

4. CASA DE SEZIM
Hotel | Restaurant | Tours | Shop
R. de Sezim, 4810-909 Guimarães
sezim.pt

Casa de Sezim offers vineyard and winery tours to visitors interested in learning the secrets of their famous Vinho Verde, produced since the Middle Ages.

The property is well-known for its enormous rooms, which house an exquisite collection of French Panoramic papers from the nineteenth century, that blend in perfectly with the monumentality of the manor façade.

Casa de Sezim is open all year and features eight comfortable bedrooms, a swimming pool, a tennis court, and walking trails through the surrounding hills.

5. PALÁCIO DA BREJOEIRA
Tours | Shop | Wine Tasting
EN 101 – Pinheiros, 4950-660 Monção
palaciodabrejoeira.pt

The imposing Brejoeira Palace cannot be missed by those passing through Monção. It is a grand neo-classical building from the early nineteenth century that was designated a national monument in 1910. The palace was opened to the public in 2010, allowing visitors to enjoy the palace's beauty and hidden relics, satisfying the curiosity of many who passed outside its gates.

Apart from the palace, the chapel, garden, woods, and, of course, the vineyards and winery are all worth seeing. This estate occupies 18 hectares of vineyards planted with the Alvarinho grape variety, producing one of the region's most iconic wines.

6. SOLAR DE SERRADE
Hotel | Tours | Meals
Mazedo, 4950-280 Monção
solardeserrade.pt

Solar de Serrade is a manor house built in the mid-17th century with typical Alto Minho architecture. Visits to the vineyards and winery are available, so are wine tastings and a shop where you can purchase the estate's wine.

You can also participate in the farm's agricultural activities, use the manor's sauna and tennis court, and stroll through its gardens and chapel.

1. *QUINTA DAS ARCAS*

2. *QUINTA DA AVELEDA*

3. QUINTA DA LIXA

4. CASA DE SEZIM

5. PALÁCIO DA BREJOEIRA

6. SOLAR DE SERRADE

Beyond wine

Start your journey in Braga, a city that combines tradition with innovation and creativity. Farther south, Guimarães, the birthplace of Portugal, is an excellent example of the evolution of a medieval settlement into a modern town. Its rich building typology exemplifies the specific development of Portuguese architecture from the 15th to the 19th century through the consistent use of traditional building materials and techniques.

Some of the attractions in this privileged area include ancient manor houses and pousadas, extremely rich gastronomy, festivities and processions, and...Vinhos Verdes. Visit churches and monuments of incomparable beauty, a vibrant popular culture, music, folklore, stories, and unparalleled handcraft. Discover the Portuguese Way to Santiago, which pilgrims have taken since the 9th century through Minho on their way to Santiago de Compostela.

Outdoor Activities

Extreme sports also play an important role not only on the rivers, like rafting in Gerês, but also kitesurfing on the windy coast, next to Viana do Castelo. Enjoy the coastline's many beaches, green mountains, manor houses, monuments, and masterpieces of traditional and modern architecture. If you enjoy golf, Minho also provides excellent scenery and facilities that compete with the best in the world.

Mouth of Rio Lima, Viana do Castelo, Ponte de Lima, Braga and Bom Jesus, Guimarães , Peneda-Gerês national park, baroque churches, and the Portuguese Route to Santiago are all must-sees.

Festivities

The Great Pilgrimage of S. Torcato is carried on the first Sunday of July in the streets of Guimarães, where the allegoric processions depict scenes from the saint's life.

The Festas Gualterianas in the summer is another highlight of the religious calendar of the city that was declared a World Heritage Site by UNESCO in 2001. One of the highlights is the procession in honor of St. Gualter.

May 3rd is a municipal holiday in Barcelos city and a sacred day to the Lord of the Crosses.

2. Douro

Land of the famous Port wine, Douro also produces world-class dry reds, whites, and rosés. All because of talented winemakers that have learned to bring out the best of a unique region recognized by UNESCO as World Heritage.

The famous terraced vineyards along the Douro River, positioned in the northeast of the country and surrounded by mountain ranges, are the result of human effort in producing quality wine under extreme conditions. The schist soil adds to the producer's difficulties but is essential in providing the sugar and coloured concentrated musts that offer the region's wine its distinct taste and aroma.

For centuries, Douro growers have focused on producing highly acclaimed fortified Ports, but in recent years, the region has gained recognition for its red and white wines. Therefore, two distinctive DOCs belong to the same region: Port and Douro's unfortified wines.

The Douro sub-regions are organized in Baixo Corgo in the west, Douro Superior in the east, and Cima Corgo in the center, each with its altitude and sun exposure:

Baixo Corgo (west) is influenced by the Atlantic Ocean, bringing precipitation and moisture to the soil, which creates the ideal setting to produce both Port and table wines.

Cima Corgo (center), where the weather is described as "Mediterranean", grapes have higher sugar concentrations, making them ideal for vintage production.

Douro Superior (east), where summer is intense, provides the requirements to produce fortified Moscatel, sparkling, and white wines.

The red wines made from *Touriga Nacional, Tinta Roriz,* and *Barroca* grapes are typically robust and full-bodied, and they often spend time aging in oak barrels. White wines, on the other hand, use grapes such as *Malvasia Fina, Gouveio, Rabigato,* and *Viosinho.*

Port Wine

Port is widely regarded as the best-fortified wine in the world due to its distinct attributes: intense aromas, a long finish, high alcohol content (19 - 22%), and a wide range of sweetness and color.

Surprisingly, Port rose to international prominence only in the eighteenth century, when Britain restricted French wine imports during the War of the Spanish Succession. The market void was quickly filled by "England's oldest ally," and the Methuen Treaty of 1703 stated that Portuguese wines would be given preferential treatment in the British market, with lower taxation.

Recognizing the importance of regulating all stages of Port wine production, the Portuguese authorities, led by *Marquês de Pombal,* established the Douro as the world's first protected designation of origin in 1756. Since then, Port wine only can be legally produced in this region.

Port vineyards were classified from A to F based on strict requirements such as soil type, vineyard location, grape variety, vine maturity, elevation, and sun exposure. Several grape varieties stand out among the 82 legally accepted types: *Touriga Franca, Touriga Nacional, Tinta Barroca, Tinta Amarela, Tinto Roriz,* and *Tinto Cão.*

The Douro vineyard region is extremely hot during most of the year, and since many Ports require at least two years of maturation, wine barrels began to be shipped down the river stream to Villa Nova De Gaia, a seaside town near Porto with a cool and humid climate. Port merchants quickly recognized Vila Nova de Gaia's strategic importance, and many aging lodges were built to age the wines.

In England, port wine became increasingly popular. However, frequently the wine had "gone bad" due to the fermentation that occurred during the long sea voyages from Portugal. The need to satisfy such a massive market prompted the development of an inventive solution: add a little cognac to ensure the wine's longevity.

Methods of production evolved, and it wasn't until the mid-nineteenth century that Port became the sweet-fortified wine we know and love today.

Types of Port

The tonality of the various types of red Port wine can range from dark purple to light gold, and any color in between can appear (red, brown, gold, and light gold). White Port, on the other hand, can have a variety of colors (light yellow to bright white), all closely related to the winemaking process. The process of aging a Port Wine can be accomplished in two distinct ways: in *bottle* and in *wood*.

Aged in bottle

When compared to wood-aged wines, this method produces a less tannic and smoother wine on the palate. The Port is aged in sealed glass bottles without being exposed to air (reductive aging), which causes the wine to lose its color very slowly throughout the process.

Vintage is a full-bodied, high-quality red wine that softens after a few years in the bottle. The Vintage is made from a single harvest and is bottled between July of the second and December of the third year after harvesting. Even though it can be consumed immediately, vintage wine is typically stored in cellars for up to 40 years. The Port and Douro Wines Institute (IDVP) in Portugal oversees the rules to recognize and categorize Port wines as Vintage.

LBV (Late Bottled Vintage) displays excellent aging potential because it is blended from several single harvest wines. It is typically aged in oak or stainless-steel tanks that allow for a slow oxidative process. After harvesting, LBV is packaged between July of the fourth year and December of the sixth year.

Crusted is made from a blend of multiple harvested wines and bottled after three to four years in wood. Because of its unique characteristics, it is normal for this wine to develop sediments (coating) in the inside walls of the bottle.

Ruby is named after the precious gemstone, and the wine is considered youthful, full-bodied, and fruity. The ruby color is the result of a three-year aging process in wooden casks with almost no oxidation. Within this category, you can also find *Ruby Reserva*, which is made from high-quality wine blends to provide extra complexity and fruity flavors when compared to a regular Ruby.

Aged in wood

These Ports are made from three-year-old blends aged in cask with several barrel transfers to force oxidation, sedimentation. This is called the racking process, which will gradually brighten the wine into a golden color. The tonality of the wines slowly becomes brownish as they mature, and the fragrances ring a bell of dehydrated fruits and wood.

Tawny is a sweet Port typically served as dessert and is made from red grapes aged in wooden barrels from three-year-old wine blends. This method involves exposing the wine to oxygen, which accelerates oxidation and aids in the development of the dry fruity flavor and the wine's distinctive golden color.

The official age designation categories are 10, 20, 30, and over 40 years, that represent the average years of aging in wood from the various harvests that comprise the Tawny.

If there is no age indication, it means you have a basic blend of wood-aged Port that has been in barrel for at least two years.

It's worth noting that the best Tawny is called *Reserva* and is made from a blend of five to seven-year-old wines. The color of a *Reserva* can range from red to brownish, depending on the winemaking process used.

Colheita is a sweet Port aged in wooden casks for a minimum of seven years from single harvest grapes. In contrast to Tawnies, the *Colheita* label specifies the year of harvest as well as the date of bottling. Because of the type of information on the label, people frequently confuse *Colheita* with Vintage Port. The difference between them, however, is clear: *Vintage* is bottled 18 months after harvest and will continue to mature in bottle, whereas *Colheita* is aged in wooden barrels for 20 years or more before being bottled.

Branco is made from white grapes and can be produced in a variety of styles depending on the level of sweetness and the length of aging. When White Ports are aged in wood for an extended period, the color darkens to the point where it is difficult to tell whether the original wine was red or white.

Young white ports are frequently drunk as an appetizer or even in cocktails, whereas older white ports are best served chilled on their own and are typically used for dessert.

In white wines, you can also find the *Reserva*, a high-quality Port made from blends that have been aged in wood for at least seven years. Its distinguishing features are its golden color and long-lasting flavor.

White Port is classified into three types based on its sweetness level: i) *Lágrima*, ii) *Doce*, and iii) *Seco*.

i) Lágrima (teardrop) is a very sweet Port wine with a sugar content of more than 130g per liter, typically made from a blend of 2-5-year-old wines. Lágrima derives its singular name from the thickness of the liquid, which resembles a teardrop when running down a glass wall.

ii) Doce (Sweet) is made from a blend of multiple aged wines, it has varying yellow tones and contains 90-130g of sugar per liter.

iii) Seco (Dry) has the lowest sugar content of any white wine, at 40-65g per liter.

Without Aging

Rosé is technically a Ruby port fermented using the techniques of rosé wines, where the reduced exposure to the grape skins contributes to the distinct pink color. It is the most recent variation in the Port Wine world, released only in 2008 by Taylor Fladgate Partnership Company. It is considered a very fresh and versatile wine.

Wine trails

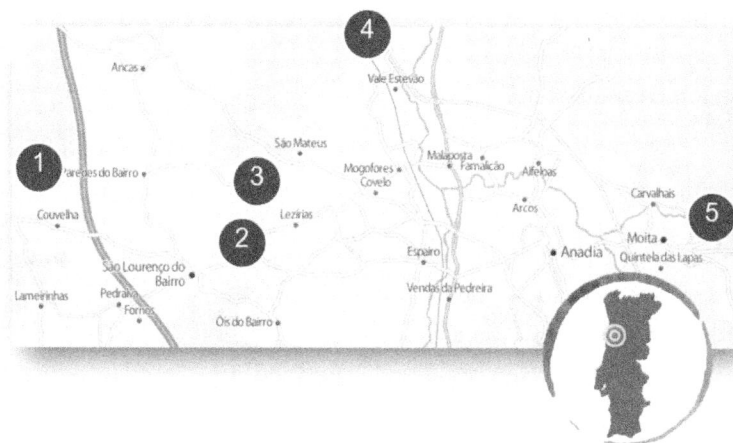

1. QUINTA DA PACHECA
Hotel | Restaurant | Tours | Shop
Cambres, 5110-424 Lamego
quintadapacheca.com

Quinta da Pacheca is one of the Douro region's oldest wine estates, and it is famous for being the first "Quinta" to bottle its wine brand. The property's heart is an 18th-century manor house restored and converted into a Boutique Hotel in 2009, offering visitors a wide range of gastronomic and oenological activities that blend rural charm with modern comfort.

After the winery tour, you can enjoy a traditional meal at the restaurant or visit the wine shop to purchase exquisite regional products and Quinta da Pacheca wines.

2. QUINTA DO VALLADO
Hotel | Restaurant | Tours | Shop
Vilarinho dos Freires, 5050-364 Peso da Régua
quintadovallado.com

Established in 1716, Quinta do Vallado is one of the oldest and most famous Douro Valley "Quintas," producing wine for the well-known Ferreira Port House for many years.
The property has 13 rooms well equipped and stands on the banks of the Corgo River, close to the town of Peso da Régua, The estate has a beautiful swimming pool and provides a variety of activities such as walks, bicycle rides, boat trips, fishing sessions, picnics, cooking classes, and wine tastings.

3. QUINTA DO CRASTO
Restaurant | Tours | Shop
Gouvinhas, 5060-063 Sabrosa
quintadocrasto.pt

Quinta do Crasto is a 130-hectare estate on the Douro River's right bank, between Régua and Pinhão. The estate's swimming pool, designed by renowned Portuguese architect Souto Moura, has been the subject of numerous visits and international media reports in recent years due to its exceptional location just above the Douro River.

Quinta do Crasto provides a variety of activities, including wine tastings, traditional meals in the restaurant, and boat rides on the Douro River. All programs conclude with a visit to the wine shop, where you can purchase Quinta do Crasto regional products.

4. QUINTA DO PÉGO
Hotel | Restaurant | Tours | Shop
EN 222, Valença do Douro, 5120-493 Tabuaço
quintadopego.com

Quinta do Pégo is situated in the Douro sub-region of Cima Corgo, near the town of Pinhão, in the heart of the UNESCO World Heritage Site. Aside from traditional wine tours, the estate also has a modern four-star hotel rebuilt from the ground up in 2009.

You can enjoy a nice traditional meal at the restaurant or relax in the pool while admiring the exceptional panoramic view of the Douro region's terraces.

The property has received the Best Wine Tourism award in the "Accommodation" category.

5. QUINTA DO SEIXO
Tours | Picnic | Shop
Valença do Douro, 5120-495 Tabuaço
sandeman.com

Sandeman's Quinta do Seixo Wine Centre stand in the heart of the Douro Valley, with an incredible view of the river and its steep terraced vineyards. Following the Douro River from Régua to Pinhão, you'll come across 99 hectares of vineyards planted with traditional Douro grape varieties used to make Port and Douro DOC Wines.

At the winery, you'll learn all about the production methods that have evolved over the centuries, resulting in a perfect blend of tradition and modernity.

For outdoor activities, you should not miss a picnic at the vineyard while enjoying the panoramic view of the valley and the river.

Quinta do Seixo has received numerous wine industry awards, including "Best New Private Project" from Turismo de Portugal and "Best of Wine Tourism" in the "Architecture, Parks, and Gardens" categories, to name a few.

1. QUINTA DA PACHECA

1. QUINTA DA PACHECA

2. QUINTA DO VALLADO

3. QUINTA DO CRASTO

4. QUINTA DO PÉGO

3. QUINTA DO SEIXO

Port wine cellars

Port is made from grapes farmed and processed in the Douro region. The wine is then fortified by adding *aguardente*, a neutral grape spirit that stops fermentation while leaving residual sugar in the wine and increases the alcohol concentration. Before being bottled and exported to various markets throughout the world, the wine is held and aged, sometimes in barrels stored in a Lodge (meaning "cellar"), as is the case in Vila Nova de Gaia, near Oporto.

Most of the port lodges are from the 1700s and 1800s and are quite attractive, complete with historic cellars, antique casks, and spectacular river views.

Here, you'll taste the primary port wine styles, including White Port, Ruby, LBV, Tawny, and Vintage Port, and learn the various delights of Port today.

WORLD OF WINE (WOW)

Rua do Choupelo 39, 4400-088 Vila Nova de Gaia
Opens daily 10:00- 01:00
wow.pt

WOW is a new attraction situated in the heart of Vila Nova de Gaia's historic district, a deserved tribute to the Portuguese culture.

The Fladgate Partnership firm invested more than 100 million euros in this audacious project, which encloses a total area of 55,000 square meters. It contains five "Experience museums", eight restaurants and cafes, an exhibition space, a wine school, several event spaces, shops, and a stunning central square with a magnificent view of the Douro River and Porto city.

CÁLEM

Avenida de Diogo Leite, 344, Vila Nova de Gaia
Opens daily May- Oct. 10-19; Nov- Apr 10 – 18
calem.pt

Among the more than 40 Port Wine labels, Porto Cálem, launched in 1859, is one of the most well-known. Almost every Portuguese is familiar with the brand, a market leader in the country, particularly for its Velhotes Tawny, Ruby, and White.

The tour begins with a visit to the museum, where you can learn more about the Douro River Region, Port wine production, and

the history of Cálem House. Then, it's time to head to the cellars
to discover the distinct qualities of each type of Port.

SANDEMAN
Largo Miguel Bombarda 47, 4400-222 Vila Nova de Gaia
Open daily: Mar-Oct10-12:30 &14-18/Nov-Feb 9:30-12:30/14-
17:30
sandeman.com

The House of Sandeman invites you to an experience filled with
mystery, in a setting that blends a classic yet cosmopolitan
environment. Located across the Douro River, the granite
building dated from 1797 gazes at the historic center of Porto.
The Sandeman Museum takes visitors to London in 1790, when
a young Scotsman named George Sandeman decided to start
marketing Port and Sherry wines.
"Sandeman, the art of a brand" is an engaging exhibition that
brings the company's history to life through an astonishing
collection of paintings, pictures, ceramics, antique bottles, and
other artifacts.

OFFLEY

Rua do Choupelo 54, 4400-174 Vila Nova de Gaia
Opens every day from Mar to Oct: 10 –12:30 & 14-16
cavesvinhodoporto.com/eng_offley

The company was founded in 1737 by William Offley with the help of Joseph James Forrester, a key player in Port history. If you're lucky enough to visit during its open season (November to February), you'll get a glimpse inside one of the city's oldest and most significant port houses.

Tours of the cellars are available, where you can learn all about Baron Forrester's life while looking at the barrels aging the precious Port wine.

TAYLOR'S

Rua do Choupelo nº 250, 4400-088 Vila Nova de Gaia
Opens Monday to Sunday: 10 – 18
taylor.pt

At Taylor's, you'll have the chance to learn about the remarkable history of the company - now in its fourth century - one of the oldest Port companies.

Guests will sample two Port wines at the end of the tour: Extra Dry White and Late Bottled Vintage (LBV). After that, you can chill on the patio that offers stunning views of the city.

RAMOS PINTO

Av. Ramos Pinto, n.º 400 - Vila Nova de Gaia
May-Oct daily & Apr (Mon-Fri): 10-18; Nov-Mar (Mon-Fri): 9-17
ramospinto.pt

Ramos Pinto stands out among the Port buildings on the main street, housed in a lovely yellow structure founded by Adriano Ramos Pinto in 1880. A visit to the cellars also includes an entrance to the museum, which exhibits a collection of art and artifacts from the house's long history. The tour concludes with a sampling of two Port wines, a red and a tawny, served in a lounge area with barrels as tables.

Beyond wine

Douro River Cruise

Indulge yourself on a boat trip to enjoy the beautiful sights of the many wine estates set on the Douro River margins. The journey along this magnificent river will take you back to the 19th century when this route was used for transporting large casks of wine from the farms way down to the coastal towns of Porto and Vila Nova de Gaia.

There are many options you can follow. From taking a *Rabelo* boat for a short trip to staying in a boat hotel for a few days. Whatever choice you make, the awesome terraced hillsides of the Douro valley will simply take your breath away.

Train trips

You may not have been privileged to ever travel on steam and diesel trains as they did back in the early '20s, but this is about to change as you embark on a trip along the Douro line that passes through 26 tunnels and 30 bridges alongside the river. Relax and appreciate the 30 Km/hr speed ride and let your adventurous side be set free to explore the stunning natural beauty that the region has to offer.

Gastronomy

When you sit at a table in the Douro, you must understand the level of care and standards poured into making delicious regional dishes, from the mouthwatering bôla, sausages, cheese made from cow and sheep milk to the Parma ham, the variety is abundant. Enjoy the traditional lamb stew, river fish, eel stew combined with "malandrinho rice" and oven-baked potatoes. Leave room to top up the meals with delicious convent sweets, olive oil cookies, sweet corn, cavacas, Teixeira biscuit, and Santa Clara pastries.

Festivities

Here, festivals here last all year, and there isn't a week that goes by without the sound of music and festivities heralding the celebration of one patron or another. Main festivals include the Lanzarim Carnival in Lamego, as well as Marian pilgrimages like Our Lady of Socorro (Peso da Régua), Our Lady of Remédios and Our Lady of Pena (Mouçós, Vila Real).

3. Dão & Bairrada

Dão is placed in the center north of Portugal (Beira Alta) in a region protected from the chilly Atlantic winds and severe continental climate, helping to create the perfect conditions for elegant red and white wines with balanced acidity and aroma. Soils are low on fertility due to their schist and granite composition.

The region is full of contrasts within its mountain walls: chilly in the north and east, warmer in the west. It is full of hills and deep valleys, forests, and mountain slopes. Climatically, the winters are cold and damp, and summers are generally sunny, warm, and dry.

The vineyards lie high in the hills, at an average of 500m above sea level, enabling generous sun exposure that allows perfect ripeness. These conditions confer Dão wines an inherent balance of bright and mineral acidity combined with a wonderful fragrance, character, and intensity.

Red wines age very well and are typically full-bodied with flavors of earl grey tea, black cherry, and cocoa provided by the *Tinta Roriz, Touriga Nacional, Alfrocheiro,* and *Jaen* grape varieties. On the other hand, white wines are produced from *Cercial, Bical, Encruzado, Verdelho,* and *Malvasia Fina* varieties that give a fruity flavor associated with lemon and baked apple.

Note that in the northwest part of Dão stands a granitic region called *Lafões* is known for producing wines high on acidity, like the nearby Vinho Verde region. Red wine varieties are *Jaen* and *Amaral* while white wines come from *Cerceal, Arinto, Dona Branca, Rabo de Ovelha*, and *Esgana Cão* grapes.

Bairrada stands between the Atlantic Ocean and the mountainous Dão region in the Beira Litoral. With warm temperatures, rainy winters, and chilly summers, the climate can be classified as "marine" due to the influence of the Atlantic Ocean.

Despite being a hilly region, most of the vines are planted on flatter lands, where the sandy or clay-limestone soils influence the style of the wine produced.

Bairrada's ADN is the red grape variety *Baga*, which is frequently planted in clayey soils that help to create the wine's vivid colors, fruity flavors, and longevity. However, in recent years, well-known foreign grape types such as Syrah, Merlot, and Pinot Noir have gained popularity and coexisted alongside local varieties.

White wines are blended from local and international types cultivated in the region's sandy soils, giving the wine a delicate and fragrant quality. *Fernão Pires* is the most widely planted grape variety, but *Cercial, Arinto, Rabo de Ovelha*, and *Chardonnay* are also widely planted.

Bairrada has a long history of producing sparkling wine using the classic bottle fermentation method, which is growing in popularity in the twenty-first century. Around 65 percent of the country's sparkling wine production is produced in this region. Typically, these wines may have the fragrance of *Fernão Pires* grapes or the steelier flavors from *Cercial, Arinto, and Bical* varieties.

The average farm size in the region is typically small, which led local producers to create cooperatives that increased scale. Smaller companies have recently begun to commercialize *Vinhos de Quinta* (farm wines), portrayed by low volume and experimentation by the winemaker.

Wine trails

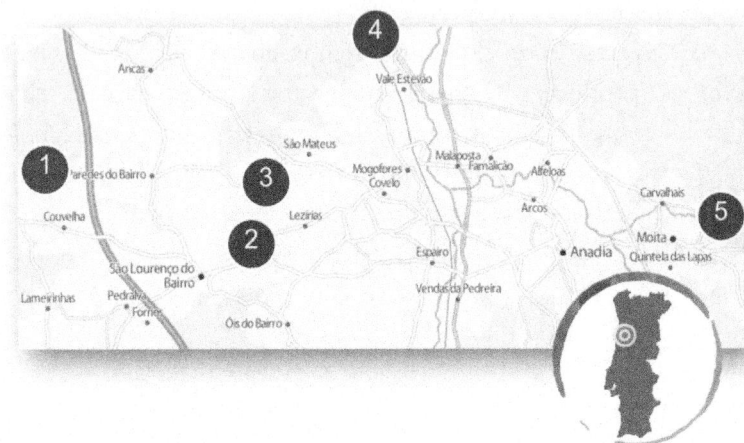

1. LUIS PATO
Hotel | Tours | Meals | Shop
Rua da Quinta Nova, 3780-017 Amoreira da Gândara
luispato.com

This family-owned estate has been producing wine since the 18th century, and the Pato family was the first winegrowers in the region to bottle its branded wine in 1970. A visit to the Quinta do Ribeirinho property will make you feel like a member of the family, as you'll have access to the family's wine library

and the *basement*, where the temperature is maintained using a method of "natural air conditioning."
Stay after the wine tour for newly released wine tasting and relics that are no longer available on the market.

2. QUINTA DO ENCONTRO
Restaurant | Tours | Tasting | Shop
R. S. Lourencinho, 3780-907 São Lourenço do Bairro
quintadoencontro.pt

Quinta do Encontro is found in São Lourenço do Bairro, in the Bairrada region. The modern building houses the winery and restaurant dominates the property landscape, surrounded by beautiful vineyards.
The wine tours stimulate visitors' senses by combining words and music with the distinct aromas of wine production. Stay for lunch or dinner after the tour and enjoy the Mediterranean-influenced cuisine, which pairs perfectly with Quinta's wines.

3. CAMPOLARGO
Hotel | Tours | Meals | Shop
Quinta S. Mateus, 3780-180 São Lourenço Bairro
campolargovinhos.com

Campolargo wine state has more than 170 hectares that produce some of the finest wines from the Bairrada region.
Besides the winery tour, you can enjoy outdoor activities at the vineyards and pine woods surrounding the main building. However, if you just prefer to relax and enjoy the charming ambiance of the property, stay at the Casa de Mogofores, the family-run guesthouse that allows you to spend the night surrounded by the Nature.

4. ALIANÇA MUSEUM
Museum | Tasting | Meals | Shop
Rua do Comércio, nº 444, 3781-908 Sangalhos
bacalhoa.pt/enoturismo/alianca-underground-museum

As the name points out, this an underground facility where you will find nine permanent collections covering a wide range of subjects, such as ceramic tiles, archeology, ethnography, paleontology, mineralogy, and even Indian culture. Visitors immerse in a one-of-a-kind atmosphere that will stimulate all their senses.

Aliança's wines, combined with local gastronomy, are the ideal starting point for a spectacular cultural tour of the museum that will make your event unforgettable (book in advance).

5. SOLAR DE SÃO DOMINGOS
Tasting | Museum | Meals | Shop
Rua Elpídio Martins Semedo, 42, 3780-473 Moita
cavesaodomingos.com

Since 1937, the Caves Solar de São Domingos is producing sparkling wines, old spirits, and table wines. The modern vinification center was inaugurated in 2006, allowing the transformation of 1,000 tons of grapes from the company's proprieties.

Its cellars house over two million bottles of sparkling wine, wine bottles, and hundreds of French oak barrels used to age the world's most famous wine-derived spirits.

The beauty of the galleries excavated in the rock, the millions of bottles, and the original tasting room from the early 20 th century, will take your breath away at this one-of-a-kind location.

1. LUIS PATO

1. LUIS PATO

2. QUINTA DO ENCONTRO

3. CAMPOLARGO

4. ALIANÇA MUSEUM

5. SOLAR DE SÃO DOMINGOS

Beyond Wine

Bairrada belongs to the Beira Litoral province, home to the historical city of Coimbra, famous for housing Portugal's oldest university. The city stands on a hill near Rio Mondego, and it is a charming place filled with ancient alleys and lanes widely spread around the university building, which is a "must-see."

The coastline of Beira is well preserved, with pine forests and sandy dunes leading into the Atlantic Ocean. You should spend some time exploring the coast towns, from the touristy Figueira da Foz to the lovely lagoon village of Praia de Mira. Aveiro, known as the "Portuguese Venice" due to its network of canals, is one of the most admired provincial towns in Portugal.

Outdoor Activities

Near Coimbra, you can visit the most extensive Roman site in Portugal (Conímbriga), the Montemor-o-Velho castle, the Buçaco forest, or the lovely "Spa Town" of Luso, ideal for relaxing after a day of fun and excitement.

Traveling northeast, you'll pass through the impressive Arouca convent and the mountain ranges of Freita and Arada, both dotted with remote villages blended into beautiful landscapes dominated by Nature that spread east until reaching the Serra da Estrela Mountain range. The highest point in continental Portugal, the only ski course in the country, the confluence of two important rivers, and an unexpected "alpine type" landscape can be seen here.

4. Lisboa & Tejo

Lisboa

This wine region is positioned north of Lisbon, where traditional and international varieties coexist to produce a diverse range of wines ranging from citric and floral whites to aromatic and tannin-rich reds.

The weather is mild due to the Atlantic influence, with cool summers and mild winters. Airstreams are a prominent feature near the coast, putting pressure on the vines to ripen their grapes. As one travels inland, the mountain ranges protect the vineyards planted on the slopes from the winds.

Since the nineties, Lisboa has invested heavily in the vineyard redesign to reach a new status in the winemaking panorama. The region formerly known as *Estremadura* is now recognized for its excellent quality-price ratio.

Lisboa wine region is composed by nine Denominations of Origin: in the south Colares, Bucelas, Carcavelos, in the centre Óbidos, Torres Vedras, Lourinhã, Alenquer, Arruda, and in the north stands Encostas d'Aire.

In the **south**, Colares is considered a "small jewel" (less than 10.000 bottles per year), where *Ramisco* grapes are planted on vines that snake along with the limestone soil and sandy dunes to reach for protection from the harsh ocean winds. The wines produced in this extreme environment can age well and achieve a balance of fresh acidity and high tannins. Also, in the south, the Bucelas Denomination of Origin produces white wines from *Arinto* grapes, a product highly regarded by European consumers since the 16th century. The characteristics of this wine, also known as "Lisbon Hock" (dry white wine), include balanced acidity, floral aromas, and the ability to age well.

As a result of significant investments in vineyard modernization and grape variety selection, the region's best DOC wines come from the **central area**. *Tinta Roriz, Castelo, Touriga Nacional, Trincadeira,* and *Tinta Miúda* are red grapes commonly used and frequently blended with international varieties, such as *Cabernet Sauvignon* or *Syrah*. In terms of white wines, the grape varieties most used in this region are *Fernão Pires, Arinto, Vital,* and *Seara-Nova*.

Alenquer produces some of the region's best red wines, known for being aromatic, elegant, tannin-rich, and capable of aging well in bottle. White wines are considered citric and fresh.

Encostas D'Aire, the region's largest Denomination of Origin, is positioned to the **north** and is known for a wide range of varieties, including *Baga, Aragonez, Chardonnay, Cabernet Sauvignon, Castelo, Touriga Nacional, Trincadeira Arinto, Malvasia Fina, and Fernão Pires*. The impact of this intriguing blend is present in the wine profile that has gained body, color, and intensity in recent years.

Tejo

The region named after Iberia's longest river, the Tejo, is situated east of Lisboa. Tejo can be described by high fertility and mild climate, allowing extensive agriculture, with rice, olive trees, and vineyards filling the vast plains.

Moving away from the river, you'll come across Bairro and Charneca, regions that are significantly hillier and drier than the riverside land (Lezíria), allowing the production of wines that are more focused on quality than quantity.

The Bairro uplands are situated north and east of the Tejo, where hills and planes alternate until they reach the foothills of the Serra dos Candeeiros and Serra de Aire Mountain ranges, which border the Lisboa area.

Charneca is a region southeast of the Tejo influenced by the neighboring Alentejo's dry and hot climate. The soils are sandy, and vine productivity is low but high in quality, with grapes ripening early in the year. The terroir is noticed in the wines: young, aromatic reds with soft tannins and fruity whites with floral aromas.

Local farmers are known for the ability to create unique wines by combining traditional grape varieties from the region, such as *Castelo* or *Trincadeira*, with external grape varieties, such as *Merlot, Cabernet Sauvignon, or Touriga Nacional*. There is less "flexibility" in white wine because the main variety used is *Fernão Pires*, sometimes blended with other grape varieties like *Tália, Trincadeira das Pratas, Arinto*, or even *Chardonnay*.

Wine Trails

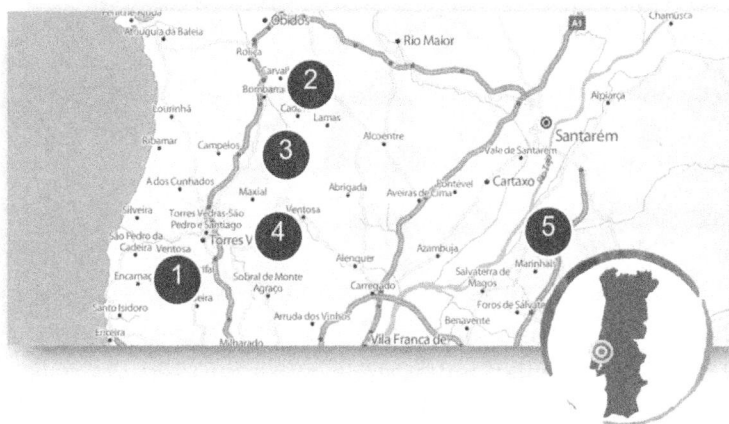

1. ADEGA MÃE
Tours | Tasting | Shop
Estrada Municipal 554, 2565-841 Torres Vedras
adegamae.pt

Adega Mãe spreads over 40 hectares of vineyards that produce annually over 1.5 million liters of white, red, and roses wines. The winery equipment fuses modern technology and traditional methods harmoniously. Over 150 American and French Oak barrels carefully selected to ensure perfect wine aging are displayed inside the "Time Room," an area dedicated to wines of noble character.

Feel free to explore the winery's heart, learn about the white and red wine presses, and marvel at the opulence of the fermentation tanks. Also accessible to visitors are the laboratory and the tasting room with a stunning vineyard view.

2. QUINTA DOS LORIDOS & BUDDHA EDEN
Restaurant | Tasting | Shop
Carvalhal 2540-480 Bombarral
bacalhoa.pt/quintas/quinta-dos-loridos

In the heart of the Óbidos region and with a history dating back to the XV Century, the Quinta dos Loridos estate is a unique place, where tranquility and nature play a special role.
Within the property, you'll find the largest oriental garden in Europe, the Buddha Eden, created in response to the Banyan Buddhas' destruction in Afghanistan.
Don't miss out on the 700 hand-painted terracotta soldiers, a central lake with KOI fish (Japanese carp), and sculpted dragons rising out of the water.

3. QUINTA DO GRADIL

Restaurant | Tours | Shop
EN115 Vilar 2550 - 073 Vilar, Cadaval
quintadogradil.wine

Quinta do Gradil, one of Cadaval's oldest estates has a long wine tradition. This property was once owned by the prime minister Marquês de Pombal, regarded as one of the most significant figures in Portuguese history.

Visitors can learn all about the wine-growing process from the vineyards to the cellar and finally to the tasting room.

Other attractions at Quinta do Gradil include a wine shop, restaurant, horseback riding, harvest events, birdwatching, an aqueduct, a chapel, and a mill.

4. CASA SANTOS LIMA

Tours | Tasting | Shop
Quinta da Boavista, 2580-081 Aldeia da Galega da Merceana
casasantoslima.com

Casa Santos Lima is a family-owned business dedicated to the production, bottling, and distribution of table wines. It is the largest producer of *Vinho Regional Lisboa* and one of the most awarded Portuguese wineries in international wine competitions.

Most of Casa Santos Lima's vineyards are located in Alenquer, 45 kilometers north of Lisbon, in a region where wine production dates back centuries.

The rural landscapes are breathtaking, with vineyards planted on gentle slopes at altitudes ranging from 100 to 220 meters, benefiting from excellent sun exposure and a climate slightly tempered by the nearby Atlantic Ocean.

5. CASA CADAVAL
Tours | Tasting | Horse Riding
Rua Vasco da Gama, 2125-317 Muge
casacadaval.pt

Casa Cadaval is placed 80 kilometers north of Lisbon, on the Tagus River's left bank. Their facilities include a beautiful wine boutique where you can sample wine while admiring the rural scenery.

The property is also well-known for being one of the world's oldest Lusitano horse breeders. The estate's stables include indoor and outdoor riding arenas as well as a viewing gallery to experience the horses' precision and ability.

The property offers a variety of activities, including wine tasting, farm tours, equestrian baptism, bird watching, and Tagus River cruises.

1. ADEGA MÃE

2. QUINTA DOS LORIDOS & BUDDHA EDEN

3. QUINTA DO GRADIL

4. CASA SANTOS LIMA

4. CASA SANTOS LIMA

5. CASA CADAVAL

Beyond wine

Lisbon, Portugal's capital, is at the heart of this multi-layered region that caters to a vast range of tastes and senses. Even though the city has had so many influences from various cultures over time, Lisbon still has a traditional feel in every historic neighborhood. Take a walk across the Pombaline grid in Baixa district streets that lead to Praça do Comércio, just in front of the Tagus River, to find beautiful city spots. Belém is a must-see in this touristy site. The area, which is rich in World Heritage monuments, harmoniously blends modern leisure spaces and medieval quarters.

A fascinating tour is the coastline route between Lisbon and the mystical village of Sintra, passing through the historical towns of Estoril and Cascais, as well as Cabo da Roca, Europe's westernmost point.

Outdoor Activities

North of Lisbon, you'll find stunning natural scenery along the coast, as well as popular surf spots like Peniche and Nazaré. Scuba divers will also enjoy the clear waters that allow marine life observation and even explore sunken ships such as the San Pedro de Alcântara.

The Óbidos Lagoon also deserves a visit due to the variety of species, like water birds and shellfish, that coexist peacefully with water sports enthusiasts.

5. Setúbal

Encountered south of Lisbon and surrounded by the Atlantic Ocean and rivers Tejo and Sado, Setúbal is known for its tourism and large wine farms that play an important role in Portuguese wine history. In fact, the longest continuous vineyard in the world during the 19th Century was in Setubal with about 4.000 hectares owned by a single proprietor. In recent years, and following a modernization trend across Portuguese regions, Setúbal wine producers have been improving quality in both viticulture and winemaking due to important investments in technology and vineyard redesign.

The landscape is flat, rarely exceeding 200 meters high with sandy soils that are suited to produce high-quality grapes. Due to the Ocean proximity, the relative humidity is high (80%) and the climate is typically Mediterranean with hot summers and mild, rainy winters.

Setúbal is a peninsula with DOCs that represent only 20% of the region's production. In Palmela, you will find excellent red wines produced from the *Castelão* variety and white wines from *Arinto* and *Fernão Pires*.

Despite the great table wines, the region's jewel is the sweet and fortified Moscatel made from *Muscat* grapes and brandy, with alcohol levels reaching 16% - 22%. After waiting around three months on the skins, the wine is aged in large wooden vats from one to 20 years, helping to develop the flower and marmalade flavors typical of Setubal Muscatel wine.

The region has also become an excellent tourist destination, thanks in part to its numerous natural parks, protected by multiple associations such Arrábida Natural Park, D. Luis Saldanha Marine Park, Sado Estuary Natural Reserve, and the Protected Fossil Cliffs Area of Caparica.

Wine trails

1. CASA-MUSEU JOSÉ MARIA FONSECA
Tours | Tasting | Restaurant | Shop
R. José Augusto Coelho, nº11/13, Vila Nogueira de Azeitão
<u>jmf.pt</u>

Built in the nineteenth century, the house was restored in 1923 by Swiss architect Ernesto Korrodi and served as the Soares Franco family residence until the 1970s. The building has always been associated with the elegant image of José Maria da Fonseca due to its beautiful façade and gardens.

The Museum House tour begins with a brief history of the company, followed by a visit to the ancient wine cellars: *Adega da Mata* and *Adega dos Teares Novos*, where wines like Periquita mature, and *Adega dos Teares Velhos*, where the oldest Setúbal Moscateis rest, some with over 100 years old.

At the end of the tour, visitors can sample José Maria da Fonseca's wines and pair them with delicious regional gourmet products.

2. PALÁCIO DA BACALHÔA
Tours | Tasting | Museum | Shop
Estrada Nacional 10, 2925-901 Azeitão
bacalhoa.pt/enoturismo/palacio-bacalhoa

At the Palace and Quinta da Bacalhôa, you'll uncover a spectacular landscape that dates back to the fourteen century. Inside the palace, unique pieces from the owner's private art collection can be admired, and outside stand beautiful gardens with ancient Olive trees transplanted from the Alqueva dam. Finish this one-of-a-kind experience with a wine tasting in the Museum of Bacalhôa's artistic space.

3. CASA ERMELINDA FREITAS
Tours | Tasting | Museum | Shop

Rua Manuel João de Freitas, Fernando Pó · 2965-595 Águas de Moura
ermelindafreitas.pt

On this beautiful property, you will unveil the details of old and new winemaking processes. The Museum of Memories captures the family history dating back to the early 1920s when wine was sold in bulk (unbranded).

Old winemaking techniques are revealed through agricultural utensils, old wine presses, and several objects related to the regional traditions associated with the harvests. Outside, you can explore the 29 grape varieties used in their wines by visiting the interactive *educational vineyard*.

The winemaking center, which is open since 2016, allows visitors to witness all stages of production, from crushing to bottling. During the tour, the "winemaking laboratory" may also be visited. The *Sala de Ouro*, where the awards and distinctions of Ermelinda Freitas are displayed, plus an exhibition on cork production, are also worth a visit.

4. SERENADA ENOTURISMO
Hotel | Restaurant | Tours | Tasting | Shop

RIC 1265 - Outeiro André - Sobreiras Altas - 7570-345 Grândola
serenada.pt

Positioned in the heart of the Serra de Grândola, A Serenada has four double rooms and four suites, inserted in a landscape that stretches between the mountain range and the Atlantic Ocean.

This scenic place, surrounded by vineyards, includes a wine cellar where guests can enjoy Serra de Grândola wines. On request, light meals can be packed in picnic baskets or simply served poolside.

On the property, you will find a mix of new and old vineyards, as well as a wine cellar, all of which are key elements of "Serras de Grândola" wine production.

Wine tastings can also be organized, at the hotel Casa do Monte for both guests and visitors.

1. CASA-MUSEU JOSÉ MARIA FONSECA

2. PALÁCIO DA BACALHÔA

3. CASA ERMELINDA FREITAS

4. SERENADA ENOTURISMO

Beyond wine

The Setubal district is an excellent starting point for a holiday in the Lisbon region, where you can fully appreciate the beauty of the Tagus and Sado estuaries. These estuaries, which boast the stunning scenery of the Arrábida mountain range and its surrounding vineyards, are home to a diverse spectrum of water birds as well as the Sado's dolphins.

Setúbal, 20 miles/32 kilometers southwest of Lisbon, is within easy reach of the district's most picturesque towns, including Palmela, Sesimbra, Alcácer do Sal, and Grândola.

In the city of Setúbal, there are numerous sites and attractions to visit. The impressive 16th Century Santa Maria da Graça Cathedral and its exquisite tiles, the Gothic church of the Jesus Monastery, an archeological museum containing fascinating vestiges of Roman occupation, and the 16th Century São Filipe Castle – built by order of King Philip II of Spain in 1595 – are among these. Setubal is also home to several picturesque fishing ports and unspoiled nature reserves.

Outdoor Activities

Exploring the natural parks of the Tagus and Sado estuaries is a popular pastime for peace-seeking visitors. Palmela is particularly well-known for its wine and is home to a massive castle positioned on a hilltop with beautiful Arrábida mountain range views. Stop in Azeitão on your way to the Arrábida mountain range (on the N249 road) to sample some of the delicious, sweet wines and muscatels that this region is known for.

The picturesque fishing town of Sesimbra, sited south of the district's capital city, is the perfect example of a charming destination and is worth a visit for its beach, excellent seafood, and lovely views of the brightly colored boats that moor along its harbor. This town, a popular summer destination, stands in the foothills of the Arrábida mountain range and its nature reserve, where you can enjoy a wide range of wildlife and plants. You can get stunning views from the massive cliffs surrounding Cabo Espichel, a secluded cape west of Sesimbra.

When traveling south, stop in Alcácer do Sal to visit the magnificent Moorish castle. Also, make time to visit Sines, a lovely destination surrounded by beaches and picturesque villages thought to be the birthplace of the legendary Portuguese explorer Vasco da Gama.

Tróia is a water sports paradise and a magnificent resort to visit during your stay. This peninsular spot will inspire you with its surrounding landscape formed by the Arrábida mountain range, the Sado estuary, and miles of lovely, natural dunes. It offers visitors a selection of long, sandy beaches and transparent waters, a variety of restaurants serving superb seafood specialties, peaceful ferry trips to the city of Setubal, many tennis courts, and a beautiful golf course.

6. Alentejo

Alentejo, located in southern Portugal, is considered one of the largest and most well-known Portuguese regions due to its rich, fruity, and easy-drinking wines, produced in a hot and dry climate with extensive sun exposure throughout the year. Naturally, the best time to visit Alentejo is in April or May, when the air is still green and aromatic and before the intense heat of the summer months. The region holds vast plains, with mountains in the northeast, where the countryside greens up and the air cools down.

Soils are low in fertility and composed of granite, pink marble, schist, and limestone, which provide the ideal conditions for growing a long-lasting and resistant vine. Landscapes coexist with vines and cereal crops, creating an ever-changing canvas of color that ranges from intense green at the end of winter to deep ochre tones in the final months of summer. Here, the red wine is the supreme ruler, so it is no surprise that the main grape varieties used are *Roupeiro, Arinto, Trincadeira, Castelo, Aragonez, Anto Vaz,* and *Alicante Bouschet*. The Denomination of Origin's eight sub-regions divides into three major groups:

1) Borba, Évora, Redondo, and Reguengos, produce wines that are smooth, harmonious, and very easy to drink.

2) Portalegre, where the vines are grown on the granite slopes of the São Mamede Mountain range, each with its unique microclimate.

3) Vidigueira, Granja-Amareleja, and *Moura* are regions that suffer from a significantly hotter climate and poor, limestone-based soils.

In addition to the DOC sub-regions, Alentejo has many regional wines that can include grape varieties other than those specified in the strict DOC wine legislation, such as *Chardonnay, Syrah*, or *Cabernet Sauvignon*.

Wine trails

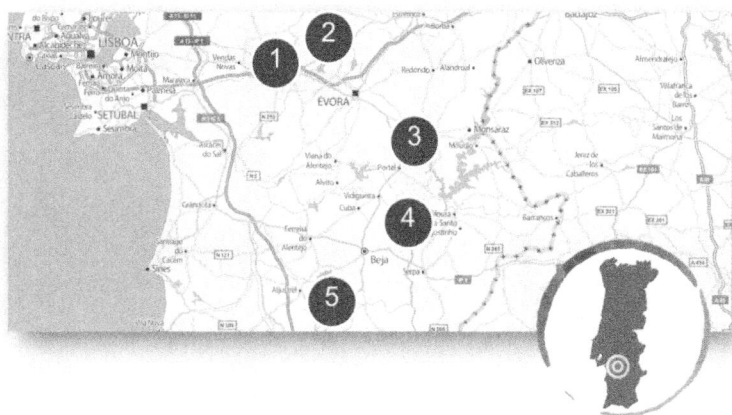

1. L'AND VINEYARDS
Hotel | Spa | Tours | Tasting
EN 4, Herdade das Valadas, 7050-031 Montemor-o-Novo
pt.l-and.com

In the heart of the Alentejo, you'll find L'AND Vineyards wine resort, perfectly integrated with the surrounding landscape dominated by the vineyards and a lake. The resort offers several suites with an open bedroom ceiling, perfect for the guests who wish to sleep under the stars with total comfort.

There are many activities to choose from: attend winemaking and organic cooking courses, visit the cellar, enjoy a traditional meal at the restaurant, or have a nice picnic at the vineyards. Finally, pamper yourself at the fully equipped SPA after a long day of excitement.

2. MONTE DA RAVASQUEIRA
Restaurant | Museum | Tours | Shop
Monte da Ravasqueira 7040-121 Arraiolos
ravasqueira.com

The estate belongs to the municipality of Arraiolos, about an hour's drive from Lisbon, and encloses a large area of typical Alentejo landscape.

Monte da Ravasqueira is dedicated to distinctive quality wine production, but it is also involved in a variety of other activities such as the production of cork, olive oil, and honey, as well as the rearing of cattle and fattening of Alentejo black pig.

Aside from visiting the vineyard or signing up for a wine course, you can also enjoy traditional Portuguese delicacies available at the restaurant or visit the Carriage Museum, which displays a private collection of harnesses and carriages from various eras and styles.

Outdoor activities include bike tours, picnics, and watersports.

3. HERDADE DO ESPORÃO
Restaurant | Tours | Shop
7200-999 Reguengos de Monsaraz
esporao.com

The Herdade, positioned in the heart of the Reguengos de Monsaraz sub-region, has unique agricultural and wine production conditions, with 700ha of vineyards, olive groves, and other crops enhanced by Organic Production.

Despite being the oldest wine tourism location in Portugal, Herdade do Esporão keeps its offer fresh with a recently refurbished wine bar, restaurant, and, of course, winery and vineyard tours.

You can walk through the vineyards and olive groves or visit the estate's historical center, which features the iconic Esporão Tower, Arch, and The Chapel of Our Lady of Remedies.

After touring the winery, cellar, and *lagares* (wine presses), unwind at the wine bar and sample the estate's wines and olive oils while admiring the spectacular view over the Caridade dam. The restaurant serves traditional Alentejo dishes such as dogfish soup or baked cod. Picnics in the vineyard, on the other hand, are an option to consider.

4. HERDADE DO SOBROSO
Hotel | Tours | Tasting | Shop
Pedrogão 7060-909 Vidigueira
herdadedosobroso.pt

The two country houses with African-inspired décor are hard to miss in *Vidigueira*, a traditional wine production region. The property has a salt-water outdoor pool with stunning views of the surrounding vineyards.

Hunting and fishing programs, photo safaris, water ski/wakeboard, kayak, windsurf, bicycle ride, boat trips, and horse-riding lessons will delight outdoor enthusiasts. Relaxing activities are also available, such as a winery and vineyard tour or eating at a restaurant that offers delicious traditional dishes.

5. MALHADINHA NOVA
Hotel | Restaurant | Tours | Tasting
7800-601 Albernoa
malhadinhanova.pt

Herdade da Malhadinha has 27 hectares of vineyard and a state-of-the-art winery where you can sample and purchase their well-known wines. The property buildings are typical Alentejo country farmhouses that combine traditional lifestyle with services that will delight even the most discerning visitors.

Outdoor activities on the property include fishing, biking, horseback riding, and hiking, but if relaxation is your goal, head to the panoramic swimming pool or pamper yourself with a Vinotherapy session at the SPA. You can dine at the gourmet restaurant, where you can sample traditional Alentejo cuisine. If you visit in August or September, you may also participate in the harvest

1. L'AND VINEYARDS

2. MONTE DA RAVASQUEIRA

3. HERDADE DO ESPORÃO

3. HERDADE DO ESPORÃO

4. HERDADE DO SOBROSO

5. MALHADINHA NOVA

Beyond wine

Near the Tagus River begins the plains that extend as far as the eye can see. While the green of the flatlands sets the pace to the north, the sun, heat, and a slower pace of life set the pace further south. At north, marshland pastures. In the vast interior, endless flatness with wheat fields waving in the wind. And on the coast, wild, beautiful beaches await to be explored.

The vastness of the landscape is dotted with time-tested cork oaks and olive trees. To absorb the magic of the place, visit a walled town, such as Marvão or Monsaraz, or uncover an ancient dolmen.

Low, whitewashed houses stand on small knolls around the hills, castles evoke battles and conquests, and yards and gardens witness the Arab influences that shaped the people and nature.

Outdoor Activities

The flat terrain facilitates hiking and cycling, though horse riding is also a popular activity. You can combine these rides with birdwatching near the dams, where a peaceful aquatic atmosphere is perfect for relaxing.

Take your time to inhale the scents of the countryside and the aromatic herbs that season the fish, seafood, and other regional delicacies, all to be accompanied by the region's excellent wines.

Towards the coast, the terrain becomes hilly and rugged, with many small, sheltered coves between the cliffs that are perfect for surfing.

7. Madeira

This Denomination of Origin with less than 500 hectares belongs to Madeira Island near the coast of Morocco, commonly known as the "Atlantic Pearl".

It is the home of the widely popular fortified wine known for its longevity, intense aromas, and distinct flavor that varies depending on the sweetness level: sweet, half sweet, half dry, and dry. The aging period typically ranges between five, ten, fifteen, and twenty years, with the latter called Vintage when made from a single grape variety.

The island's climate is *Mediterranean*, with mild temperatures all year. The soils are quite unfertile due to the volcanic nature of the island, which contributes to the wine's high acidity. As a result of the island relief irregularity, the vineyards are planted on the volcanic slopes using grape varieties such as *Tinta Mole* (80%), *Malvasia*, *Verdelho*, *Boal*, and *Sercial*.

The qualities of Madeira wine remain unaltered for many years after the bottle is opened and exposed to air, lasting for months in good conditions - a perfect solution for occasional after-dinner drinkers.

Madeira wine follows the same production techniques as Sherry and Port wine, with the addition of a neutral grape spirit (brandy) to fortify the alcohol level and stop fermentation at some point. Storage methods defy all known rules by intentionally heating ("cooking") the wine, typically in a hot attic. Origins of this practice can be traced back to the 18th century when wine suffered high temperatures during long sea voyages to reach external markets. People noticed that due to prolonged exposure to heat and oxygen, the wine gradually became more aromatic and richer in dried fruit flavors. With this discovery, Madeira wines were now sent on long journeys to perfect their qualities. Years later, producers began to replicate on land the heating conditions felt by the wine offshore with attics and heated wine containers.

For many years, Madeira has been highly regarded abroad, particularly in the United Kingdom, where the wine was considered a must-have in Court celebrations, and even used as a perfume by high-society ladies! Throughout the years, many were the personalities, statesmen, and mythical characters dazzled by this wine, of whom are emblematic examples George Washington, Thomas Jefferson, and Winston Churchill.

Napoleon made sure to stop on his way to exile to take a barrel of Madeira Wine to the island of Saint Helena and the US independence was celebrated with a toast of this magnificent wine.

Shakespeare was also not indifferent to Madeira wine attributes. In the play Henry IV, the character Falstaff sold his soul to the devil "for a cup of Madeira and a cold capon's leg."

Madeira wine was present even in the most dramatic episodes of English history: when sentenced to death for attempting to murder his brother Edward IV, the Duke of Clarence chose to die by drowning in a Madeira cask!

Wine trails

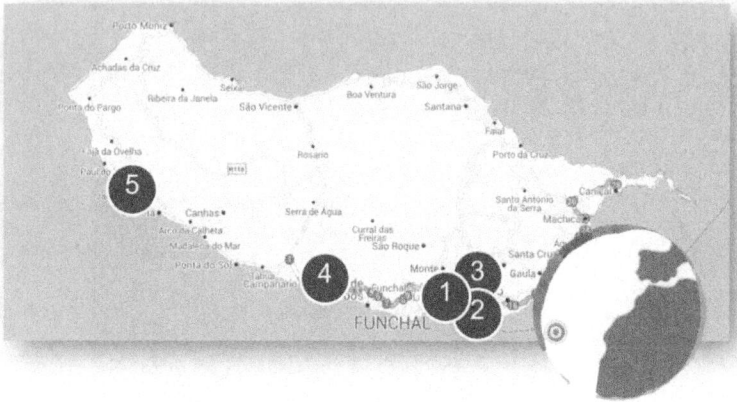

1. D'OLIVEIRAS
Tours | Tasting | Shop
Rua Dos Ferreiros 107, 9000-082 Funchal
doliveiras.pt

The Pereira D'Oliveiras offer wine tasting and tours at their gorgeous historic building dating from 1619, formerly a structure of the Jesuit College in Funchal.

The company, founded in 1820, consists of five wine producers that made D'Oliveira one of the biggest Madeira shippers in the world.

The owners have always been the D'Oliviera family, regarded as the most influential growers in the São Martinho area.

Their stock of old wines is impressive and has grown over time, either through marriage with other wine-producing families or through other business acquisitions.

2 H. M. BORGES
Tours | Tasting | Shop
Rua 31 de Janeiro, 83 9050-011 Funchal
hmborges.com

H.M. Borges was founded in 1877 by Henrique Menezes Borges, who dedicated his entire life to aging a selection of wines produced on the island. The company is now managed by the family's fourth generation.

Their winery is operating since 1924 in a historic building with approximately 1.600 square meters, positioned in the Funchal center.

At the wine tour, you will learn the company's history and every step of the Madeira Wine production. Wine tastings occur at the end of the visit in a 19th-century wood room decorated with Max Römer paintings. At the shop, you can find great deals to stock your private cellar with that special bottle of Madeira Wine.

3. BLANDY'S
Tours | Tasting | Shop
Avenida Arriaga 28, 9000-064 Funchal
blandyswinelodge.com

The company's history began when John Blandy arrived on the island in 1807, and since then, the family has played a leading role in the development of Madeira wine.

Blandy's offers visitors the chance to explore its Wine Lodge, a museum housed in a complex of old wineries. During your visit, you will notice unique artifacts and historical documents that narrate the story of the Blandy family and its wines.

The tasting sessions take place in the *Max Romer* room, where you can appreciate beautiful murals depicting the entire process from picking grapes to wine bottling, painted by a renowned German artist. The *Overnighter Room* houses the rarest wines and old wood, allowing visitors to sample wine from past centuries.

4. VINHOS BARBEITO
Tours | Tasting | Shop
*Estrada da Ribeira Garcia, Parque Empresarial de Câmara de Lobos -
Lote 8, 9300-324 Câmara de Lobos*
vinhosbarbeito.com

Vinhos Barbeito was founded in 1946 by Mário Barbeito de
Vasconcelos and is managed by family members ever since.

The visit starts with a guided tour of the winery, where you can
learn all about the winemaking process and equipment, such as
the Robotic Lagar. A guide will explain everything from grape
harvesting to acquiring the finished product while showing the
old oak casks where wines age.

Following the tour, you will have the opportunity to taste eight
wines ranging in age from 3 to 20 years in the *Tasting and
Memories Room*, a place that holds a collection of documents and
memories dating back to the company's origins.

It's advised to schedule your visit in advance.

5. QUINTA DAS VINHAS
Hotel | Restaurant | Tours | Tasting
Estrada Regional 223, nº 136, 9370-237 Calheta
qdvmadeira.com

Quinta das Vinhas is a beautiful wine hotel located in Calheta. Built from a 17th-century manor house, the property offers two outdoor pools, and small cottages spread through the vineyards. The property was born with the intent to preserve the owner's family heritage while letting visitors experience staying in a traditional Madeira farmhouse.

In 2018 the property was fully refurbished, and the cottage that stands on top of the vineyards was revamped into a restaurant and wine bar, where you can have dinner and sample a large selection of local wines.

For many years, their land was leased to the Madeira Wine Institute for experimental vineyards. As a result, Quinta das Vinhas owns a unique living library with over 70 different grape varieties, both for winemaking and eating.

Don't miss out on their guided tours and wine tasting sessions at the cellar and the vineyards.

1. D'OLIVEIRAS

2 H. M. BORGES

3. BLANDY'S

3. BLANDY'S

4. VINHOS BARBEITO

5. QUINTA DAS VINHAS

Beyond wine

Madeira is a perfect destination to visit any time; the island has mild temperatures all year long due to its mountainous landscape and privileged location in the Atlantic Ocean. Of course, there may be some rainy or windy days during the winter, but they are uncommon. The upside is that you will be able to see the island in full bloom.

The island is relatively small, but the number of places to visit and activities to participate in is far out of proportion. Madeira has much to offer, from the famous walking trails to spots with unrivaled views of the island's coast, exotic local flowers, and fruits, and some of the best places for diving in the world.

Outdoor Activities

The *levadas* are part of a network of water channels and tunnels built in the fifteenth century, during the early settlements. Tracking these water structures allow spectacular walks, sometimes for relatively easy paths, others through tunnels or walking several minutes on the edge of a cliff. And given the popularity of these walks, local authorities mapped and classified the various paths, from beginner to advanced level.

To visit Madeira and not go on a trekking expedition to the *Levadas*, is to miss out on a great adventure filled with the most beautiful landscapes you will see in your lifetime.

You can return to Funchal center by cable car, on foot, by taxi, or even better, in a ***traditional basket car***. It's one of Madeira's oldest ways of transportation, perfectly preserved over time and now transformed into a tourist attraction. This high-speed descent in a basket driven by two men who use their rubber boots as brakes will boost your adrenaline.

In ***Porto Moniz***, you can swim in crystal clear waters among volcanic rocks in the famous natural swimming pool. The entrance is free, but if you need access to the pool's facilities, you'll have to pay a small fee.

One of the most amazing viewpoints in Madeira is found in ***Cabo Girão***, Europe's highest cape. It features a skywalk, a glass platform that allows you to see the landscapes beneath your feet. The panoramic views of Funchal, Câmara de Lobos, and the endless horizon of the Atlantic Ocean make this a must-see destination on the island of Madeira.

Gastronomy

Madeira's cuisine is simply captivating. Local dishes include tasty grilled limpets, warm *bolo do caco* with garlic butter, tuna steaks with fried corn, and the famous skewer on laurel stick. The traditional drink is called Poncha, a mix of Madeira cane brandy, honey, sugar, orange, and lemon juice. It goes down like juice but goes up like brandy, so you must drink it with caution!

Festivities

The **Festa dos Compadres** kicks off Madeira Island's celebrations. It is celebrated in Santana municipality from the 5th to the 7th of February and holds an impressive parade of amusing giant figures through the streets. The festivity concept is the judgment of the *compadre* and *comadre* (grandparents), with the giant dolls serving as satire and criticism of the locals.

The **Flower Festival** celebrations occur in May when the island becomes dressed in colorful flowers. The Allegorical Flower Parade in Funchal, attended by hundreds of people, is the festival's highlight celebration.

Like other Portuguese regions, Madeira also celebrates **popular saints day** with lively and colorful street parades. These events honor St. Anthony, St. Peter, and St. John's Days on the 12th, 13th, and 23rd of June.

Madeira *celebrates wine* in September, reviving old traditions associated with this agricultural activity. The festivities begin in Funchal with Folklore Week and finish in Estreito de Câmara de Lobos with the Harvest Festival. If you need an excuse, it's an excellent opportunity to sample all the types and brands of Madeira wine.

In December, thousands of people gather around the island to experience the beautiful *New Year's Eve fireworks*, recognized in 2006 by the Guinness Book of Records as the world's largest show.

Getting the most out of
Portuguese Wine
(or any wine)

Storing

Here are some facts you should consider if you plan to invest in a cellar. Begin with the basics: it should be an open space, protected from light and extreme temperature fluctuations (acceptable between 7°C and 13°C) to prevent the wine from becoming oxidized, cooked, or developing dried cork.

Humidity represents another element to consider - the optimal range is between 60% and 75%. If the cellar is too humid, you may need to buy a dehumidifier or lime blocks to absorb humidity. On the other hand, if you need to increase air humidity, it is advised to water the floor if possible.

A convenient solution to help regulating the temperature and humidity levels is through a thermometer and a hygrometer, but you can find more expensive options like installing a refrigerated cellar, where temperature and humidity are constant and easily controlled. A standalone cellar is an excellent option to consider. It comes with its cooling system, is regulated easily, and can be adapted to your needs with sizes ranging from a 24-bottle capacity up to more than 500 bottles.

Once in the cellar, the wine must move as little as possible, so ideally, you should plan your bottle arrangement before you begin. Bottles should be displayed horizontally so that the wine stays in contact with the cork, avoiding air exposure. The most valuable bottles should be nearer to the ground since it is the coolest area in the cellar.

Leftover Wine

After your fiesta, you may have leftover wine that you want to save for a future occasion. You must realize that once a bottle is open, the oxygen begins to work its magic, and eventually, it will turn wine into vinegar.

There are several ways to preserve a partially consumed bottle, but even the cleverest methods will merely buy you a few days, or a week at best. An interesting option is spraying Nitrogen or Argon gas onto the surface of the wine before re-corking. One caveat to this method is you must leave the wine undisturbed and upright because if you jostle the bottle, you will dissipate the gas and the protection it offers. Another straightforward way to preserve wine is through a wine pump, such as a *Vac-u-vin*, which removes the oxygen from the bottle.

There are other gadgets on the market like the *Coravin* and the *Enomatic*. Both are great, especially if you want to pour small amounts from older or rare bottles, but they are expensive even if highly recommended.

Opening the Bottle

The corkscrew represents an all-important tool for opening a wine bottle. There are numerous types of corkscrews, but the best one is not always the most beautiful or expensive, but the one that works best for you.

When the cork is removed vertically, there are fewer chances of breaking it. However, if the cork shatters into the bottle, its small fragments will fall into the wine and cause an unpleasant situation, despite not harming the wine quality. A straightforward solution is to pour a small amount out of the bottle in one quick splash – that will usually take care of any stray pieces.

Still wine bottles are often sealed with foil at the top. The first step is to cut the foil with the built-in knife most corkscrews have and cut below the flange at the top of the bottle. You can remove the entire foil or just the part above the neck, either way, is acceptable. Next, clean the bottle opening with a dry cloth to eliminate mold or sediments and insert the corkscrew carefully, with the point (called worm) at the center of the cork. Screw the worm carefully not to go past the end of the cork inside the bottle and remove it by pulling it out slowly. Note that many corkscrews have a lever where you can rest against the lip of the bottle that will provide leverage.

When opening an old wine bottle, be aware that the cork may break or disintegrate. If it breaks, insert the corkscrew once again, push it against the inside wall of the neck of the bottle and gently pull the cork out. If this doesn't work, simply push it back into the bottle. You can then filter the wine through a coffee filter, cheesecloth, or decanting funnel to extract the bits of cork. To avoid breaking or disintegrating the cork, you may also use a specific set of tongs with arms that adjust to the wine's neck. Another option is to use an 'ah-so' corkscrew, which features two parallel strips of metal that you can shimmy down the sides of the cork and gently twist out.

Sparkling wine bottles should never be opened with a corkscrew. As they are under different atmosphere pressures, they require special handling for cork removal, as it may launch into the air, spill the wine, and potentially injure your guests. In sparkling wines, the cork is protected with foil and a cage that must be removed before opening the bottle. Tilt the bottle away from your guests and hold it in one hand while your other hand holds the cork to prevent it from flying off. Gently turn your hands away from each other but do not pull, as the pressure will push the cork out on its own. Ideally, you should hear a soft air escape instead of a loud 'pop'!

Ruined wine

It could be very disappointing to serve an oxidized wine bottle. If you take proper care of your wine, you will rarely ever have this problem, though you will inevitably purchase a faulty bottle. Signs of oxidation include discoloration of red wine to a faded brown, but keep in mind this is not always an issue because some wines are naturally brick-colored.

White wines will turn from pale white to brown, amber, or golden yellow and might smell off, even vinegary, with flat and strange flavors.

Another quality issue you must be careful of is cork taint, caused by bacteria that make the wine taste musty and bitter. You will immediately notice the off smell of corked wine, despite being harder to detect in chilled white wines.

All the above is a bottle-to-bottle situation: just because one bottle is affected doesn't mean the next one will have the same problem. So, when planning a wine tasting session, make sure you purchase more than one bottle of each wine to be on the safe side.

Serving

You don't need to be a wine expert to serve it like a pro. Considering some key principles, you can't go wrong:

- Start with sparkling as it wakes up the palate and gets people in a celebratory mood.

- Dry wines are always served before sweet wines.

- White wines should be served before red wines.

- If you are serving a rosé, serve it before reds.

- Young, lighter-bodied wines before heavier wines.

- If serving fortified wines, try to place them last. Their higher alcohol content will create palate fatigue.

One might say that there are no rules: start with the basics, but as you become more adventurous, be confident to let your imagination run wild.

Always taste the wine before pouring it for your guests to guarantee it is in good condition. Tradition says that you should customarily serve ladies first and further to that oldest lady first. If you wish to avoid unnecessary risks, simply pour in a clockwise direction, ending with the host. In any case, make sure that you can divide the bottle to have enough quantity to serve everybody at the table.

Serve the wine from the guest's right side, holding the bottle at the bottom so that the label is upright and visible. The host is always the last person to be served.

Temperature

Wine is invariably at its best when served at the proper temperatures. If a wine is too warm or cold, it will not deliver its best flavor and aromas. Above all, you should never serve wine at a temperature higher than the air in the room, as it may amplify any volatile acidity and provide an unpleasant tasting experience.

If you need to chill the wine, I recommend a simple technique: place the bottle into a bucket and cover it with ice. Then, fill it with water up to the bottle neck and wait a few minutes.

Type of Wine	Refrigeration (hours)	Reference Serving Temperature	
		Celsius (°C)	Fahrenheit (°F)
Light Reds	1	12-16	54-61
Medium-bodied Reds	–	14-17	57-63
Full-bodied Reds	–	15-18	59-64
Sparkling	4	5-10	41-50
Light Sweet Whites	4	5-10	41-50
Dry Light Aromatic Whites	2	10-12	50-54
Medium-bodied Dry Whites	1.5	10-12	50-54
Full-bodied Sweet Whites	1.5	10-12	50-54
Full-bodied Dry Whites	1	12-16	54-61

Tasting

In your mouth, several areas pick up different sensations. The tip of your tongue will pick up sweetness or saltiness; the sides detect acidity, and the far back notice bitterness. Wines offer many aromas and flavor profiles that can be described as floral, earthy, leathery, coffee, tea, and fruits like apple, strawberry, citric, cherry, or blueberry; the list goes on and on. You can even find not expecting odors, like an animal scent, smoke, or tar. The possibilities are endless, but it will be easier to express your sensations if you have a wide range of smell vocabulary.

Tasting Sequence

✓ **Pour** a small amount of wine into the glass (about 60 ml).

✓ **Observe** the color of the wine by looking at it against a white tablecloth or wall.

✓ **Smell** by placing your nose into the glass and taking a deep sniff. Report any smells you notice right away.

✓ **Swirl** the wine while keeping the glass base on the table. Swirl in quick circles, making the wine inside splash up the edges of the glass.

✓ **Smell** the wine for a second time and note the new aromas lifted after the swirl.

✓ **Taste** by taking a mouthful of wine and holding it in.

✓ **Swish** the wine into every single corner of your mouth. During this process, consider aerating by taking a little "sip" of air through your teeth and the wine in your mouth.

✓ **Spit** the wine into a prepared receptacle for this event. It can be a metal cocktail shaker, pint glass, a bucket, or a pitcher that you can spit into.

I know many people don't like to spit out their wine, but trust me, if you are attending a tasting session and want to experience more than three wines, you will have to learn to spit pretty quickly, or you won't last! Never forget that alcohol in your system impairs the ability to taste wine by dulling the palate.

Host a Wine Tasting Event

Hosting a wine tasting is a fun and relaxed way to discover new wines, expand your knowledge and socialize with others who share the passion for the good things in life. Here is a comprehensive rundown of what is needed to make it happen.

Guestlist: decide how many guests you can comfortably host and base your plans around that number. Make sure you have enough room for people to mingle and sit down if they wish.

Wine: tasting from four to six types of wine should be sufficient, as long as you provide variety. For instance, you might decide on six wines, so you could split them up by having three reds, two whites, and a rose, of whatever you prefer. Choose wines different in style, varietal, or age to set them apart. You can even prepare a themed event, like *Wines from Spain*, where guests must place on the map each wine tasted according to the attributes associated with the regions.

Glassware: based on the number of guests, try to have at least two glasses per person (one for red, one for white). If the glassware is an issue, you could go with one each in a pinch - just make sure spring water is available to rinse glasses between tastes.

Ideally, you should provide proper tasting glasses called INAO. They are relatively small because they are designed for tasting and not for drinking.

Tasting sheets: prepare a sheet for your guests to jot down their thoughts. It is a clever idea to keep at hand the price and where you purchased the wine so that your guests know where to find something they absolutely love. Bellow, you will find a tasting sheet example that includes scores, but you can always make your own based on the goals for the session.

Water for rinsing: have plenty of spring water on hand so that people may rinse their glasses if they wish. Avoid using tap water because it is chlorinated and will leave chemical residues on the glass, which may impart off-flavors. In addition, keep a case of individual water bottles on hand for people to drink.

Dump Buckets: even if you are not experienced "spitters", it doesn't mean you can't practice! Consider having dump buckets nearby to accommodate any extra wine the taster has inadvertently poured. You can use any receptacle, like the metal cup of a cocktail shaker, a disposable plastic beer cup, an ice bucket, or anything similar you have on hand. Just be sure to check the buckets regularly and empty them when necessary.

Setup: display your table or counter with the wines so that people may approach the bottles and pour them without effort. Make sure to leave some room between wines for people to linger.

Food: make sure you have something on hand for your guests to nibble. Some tasters like a small piece of bread or a saltine cracker in between tastes to neutralize their palate. Cheeses are optional, but for tasting purposes, stick to hard, salty cheeses rather than pungent or ripened, since they are difficult to pair correctly and can impart some "interesting flavors" to the wine. Furthermore, avoid spicy food and green vegetables as they can also interfere with the palate. Stick to neutral flavors and you'll be fine.

Pictures: make sure you record images, as your guests will want to remember how lovely your event was! Take some photos of the bottles to tie the whole thing together.

Keep it simple: don't overcomplicate the party as it is meant to be fun, entertaining, and social. Have background music to elevate the mood, but not so loud as people can't talk over it. You will want to encourage discussion around the wines, as each opinion is highly valid in the overall scheme of things.

Above all, just have FUN!

Happy wine tasting!

DATE:	DATE:	DATE:
WINE:	WINE:	WINE:
VINTAGE:	VINTAGE:	VINTAGE:
COLOR/APPEARANCE:	COLOR/APPEARANCE:	COLOR/APPEARANCE:
APPEARANCE SCORE: /5	APPEARANCE SCORE: /5	APPEARANCE SCORE: /5
NOSE:	NOSE:	NOSE:
NOSE SCORE: /15	NOSE SCORE: /15	NOSE SCORE: /15
MOUTH:	MOUTH:	MOUTH:
MOUTH SCORE: /20	MOUTH SCORE: /20	MOUTH SCORE: /20
CONCLUSIONS/SCORE:	CONCLUSIONS/SCORE:	CONCLUSIONS/SCORE:
FINISH/OTHER SCORE: /10	FINISH/OTHER SCORE: /10	FINISH/OTHER SCORE: /10
TOTAL SCORE: /100	TOTAL SCORE: /100	TOTAL SCORE: /100

Tasting sheet example

Final words

I'm scribbling these words in a late afternoon sitting at a table glancing at Douro River while escorted by saltine crackers creamed with Queijo da Serra and a glass of Quinta da Pacheca red wine.

I've been coming to this place for a long time. The first time I visited it, ten years ago, I was a naive wine lover eager to taste the best wines from the Douro Region. Heck, the goal was actually to find the best wine of Portugal...the "perfect wine"!

With age, wisdom kicks in, and I've understood that "perfect" is a fleeting thing, and if you are anything like me, it's often better in retrospect.

Now I realize that throughout the years, I've experienced many perfect wines. They were perfect because they chaperoned a *perfect* company, at a *perfect* place in a *perfect* moment!

Philosophical thoughts apart, one thing is sure: almost all Portuguese wines offer amazing value, being fresh citric whites gor full-bodied reds.

Hopefully, after reading this book, you will think of Portuguese wine beyond Port. Despite being an extraordinary ambassador of the country's wines, it is just the tip of the iceberg when it comes to the world of winemaking in Portugal.

The sun has now landed behind the hill. The chilly wind crosses the valley telling me it's time to retreat. I hold no resistance, as I've completed the final words of the Easy Wine Guide - Portugal.

I hope that by now, you are already scheduling your trip to Europe's most exciting wine region!

Miguel Dias

.

What Did You Think of **EASY WINE GUIDE PORTUGAL?**

Thank you for purchasing my book. I know you could have picked any number of books to read, but you picked this one, and for that, I am extremely grateful.

If you found some benefit in reading this book, I hope you could spare a minute to post a review on Amazon. It is a small but precious action for the book to reach a wide range of readers.

I wish you all the best.
Cheers!

About the author

You could say that Miguel's love of wine is in his blood. Throughout his life, regular visits to his grandfather's farm imbued him with passion for the grape. He literally learned the business from the ground up, helping with harvest and gaining practical knowledge of traditional winemaking methods as passed down through the generations in his Portuguese winemaking family.

Miguel is a certified wine consultant and the founder of Wineberia, an NPO that offers customized wine experiences in Portugal and Spain. This exciting venture allowed Miguel to immerse himself in the region's vast culture, falling in love with its traditions, wine, and cuisine.

With a stated mission to break free of commonly held wine snobbery, Miguel brings an air of simplicity to the task of wine study. Emphasizing the social and entertaining aspects of wine culture, he hopes to break down centuries of tradition into language that is easy to understand and fun to learn.

Bibliography

Barreto, António, Douro, Lisboa: Ed. Inapa

Beazley, Mitchell, A Century of Wine – The Story of the Wine Revolution, London: Octopus Publishing.

Boniface, Brian G. & Cooper, Cris, Worldwide destinations: the geography of travel and tourism, 3º Ed., Oxford: Butterworth-Heinemann.

Boniface, Priscilla, Tasting Tourism: Travelling for Food and Drink, Hampshire: Ashgate Publishing.

Correia, Luís & Ascenção, Mário Passos, "Wine Tourism in Bairrada Wine Route", in Carlsen & Charters (eds.), Global Wine Tourism – Research, Management & Marketing, Oxon: Cabi International

Costa, Adriano, "O Enoturismo em Portugal: o Caso das Rotas do Vinho", Revista da Ciência da Administração, Pernambuco. Univ.de Pernambuco

Falcão, João Marinho, "Turismo, Vinho e Gastronomia", in ITP, Novos Produtos Turísticos, Lisboa: ITP.

Gonçalves, Francisco Esteves, Portugal a wine country, Lisboa: Livros Técnicos e Científicos

Hall, C. Michael, et al., Wine Tourism around the World – Development, management and markets, Oxford: Butterworth-Heinemann.

Mayson, Richard, Os Vinhos e Vinhas de Portugal, Mem Martins: Publicações EuropaAmérica.

Nabais, António, "A vinha e o vinho: colecções e museus", in O Vinho, a História e a Cultura

Postgate, Raymond, Portuguese Wine, London: J. M. Dent & Sons.

Salvador, José A., Portugal – Vinhos, Cultura e Tradição, Rio de Mouro: Círculo de Leitores.

Salvador, José A., Os Autores dos Grandes Vinhos Portugueses, Porto: Edições

Afrontamento.

Simões, Orlando, A vinha e o vinho no século XX, Oeiras: Celta.

Simões, Orlando, "A vinha e o Vinho em Portugal: Contributos para o desenvolvimento local e regional" in Portela & Caldas, PT Chão, Oeiras: Celta

Vieira, João Martins, A Economia do Turismo em Portugal, «Biblioteca de Economia & Empresas», Lisboa: Publicações Dom Quixote

Notes to the reader

While the author of this book has made reasonable efforts to ensure the accuracy and timeliness of the information contained herein, the author assumes no liability with respect to loss or damage caused or alleged to be caused, by any reliance on any information contained herein and disclaim any and all warranties, expressed or implied, as to the accuracy or reliability of said information. The advice contained herein may not be suitable for every situation and the authors do not warrant the performance, effectiveness, or applicability of any sites listed or linked to in this book.

The author is not affiliated with any of the properties mentioned in the book, and all links are for information purposes only and are not warranted for content, accuracy, or any other implied or explicit purpose.

Copyright protection

Also available: Easy Wine Guide Spain

Printed in Great Britain
by Amazon